50 Pie Recipes for Home

By: Kelly Johnson

Table of Contents

- Apple Pie
- Cherry Pie
- Pumpkin Pie
- Pecan Pie
- Blueberry Pie
- Peach Pie
- Lemon Meringue Pie
- Key Lime Pie
- Chocolate Cream Pie
- Banana Cream Pie
- Sweet Potato Pie
- Coconut Cream Pie
- Strawberry Rhubarb Pie
- Maple Pecan Pie
- Raspberry Pie
- Buttermilk Pie
- Mincemeat Pie
- Shoofly Pie
- Chicken Pot Pie
- Beef Pot Pie
- Spinach and Feta Pie
- Quiche Lorraine
- Broccoli Cheddar Pie
- Tomato Pie
- Tofu Pot Pie
- Pear Pie
- Mixed Berry Pie
- Custard Pie
- Caramel Apple Pie
- Ginger Peach Pie
- Blackberry Pie
- Fig Pie
- Sweet Corn Pie
- Egg Custard Pie

- Almond Cream Pie
- Lemon Chess Pie
- Poppy Seed Pie
- Chocolate Peanut Butter Pie
- Peanut Butter Pie
- Apricot Pie
- Chocolate Bourbon Pecan Pie
- Maple Cream Pie
- Orange Cream Pie
- Almond Raspberry Pie
- Zucchini Pie
- Tomato Basil Pie
- Honey Pie
- Butterscotch Pie
- S'mores Pie
- Key Lime Cheesecake Pie

Apple Pie

Ingredients:

- **For the Pie Crust:**
    - 2 ½ cups all-purpose flour
    - 1 tsp salt
    - 1 tsp sugar
    - 1 cup (2 sticks) unsalted butter, chilled and cut into small cubes
    - 6-8 tbsp ice water
- **For the Filling:**
    - 6 cups peeled, cored, and thinly sliced apples (Granny Smith or Honeycrisp work well)
    - ¾ cup granulated sugar
    - ¼ cup packed brown sugar
    - 2 tbsp all-purpose flour
    - 1 tsp ground cinnamon
    - ¼ tsp ground nutmeg
    - ¼ tsp ground allspice
    - 1 tbsp lemon juice (about half a lemon)
    - 1 tbsp unsalted butter, cut into small pieces
- **For Assembly:**
    - 1 egg, beaten (for egg wash)
    - 1 tbsp sugar (for sprinkling)

Instructions:

1. **Prepare the Pie Crust:**
    1. In a large bowl, whisk together the flour, salt, and sugar.
    2. Add the chilled butter and use a pastry cutter or your fingers to work it into the flour until the mixture resembles coarse crumbs.
    3. Gradually add the ice water, one tablespoon at a time, mixing until the dough just comes together. Do not overwork.
    4. Divide the dough into two equal portions, flatten each into a disk, and wrap in plastic wrap. Chill in the refrigerator for at least 1 hour.
2. **Prepare the Filling:**

1. In a large bowl, combine the sliced apples, granulated sugar, brown sugar, flour, cinnamon, nutmeg, allspice, and lemon juice. Toss to coat the apples evenly. Set aside.
3. **Assemble the Pie:**
   1. Preheat your oven to 425°F (220°C).
   2. On a lightly floured surface, roll out one disk of dough to fit a 9-inch pie dish. Carefully transfer it to the dish, pressing it into the bottom and up the sides.
   3. Pour the apple filling into the crust, and dot with the pieces of butter.
   4. Roll out the second disk of dough and place it over the filling. Trim any excess dough and crimp the edges to seal. You can also cut the dough into strips and create a lattice top if you prefer.
   5. Brush the top crust with the beaten egg and sprinkle with sugar.
4. **Bake the Pie:**
   1. Place the pie on a baking sheet to catch any drips and bake in the preheated oven for 45-55 minutes, or until the crust is golden brown and the filling is bubbling.
   2. If the edges of the crust start to brown too quickly, cover them with aluminum foil.
5. **Cool and Serve:**
   1. Allow the pie to cool on a wire rack for at least 2 hours before serving. This helps the filling set and makes it easier to slice.

Cherry Pie

Ingredients:

- **For the Pie Crust:**
    - 2 ½ cups all-purpose flour
    - 1 tsp salt
    - 1 tsp sugar
    - 1 cup (2 sticks) unsalted butter, chilled and cut into small cubes
    - 6-8 tbsp ice water
- **For the Filling:**
    - 4 cups fresh or frozen tart cherries (thawed and drained if frozen)
    - 1 cup granulated sugar
    - ¼ cup cornstarch
    - 1 tsp lemon juice
    - 1 tsp vanilla extract
    - ¼ tsp almond extract (optional)
    - 1 tbsp unsalted butter, cut into small pieces
- **For Assembly:**
    - 1 egg, beaten (for egg wash)
    - 1 tbsp sugar (for sprinkling)

Instructions:

1. **Prepare the Pie Crust:**
    1. Follow the same instructions as for the apple pie crust.
2. **Prepare the Filling:**
    1. In a large bowl, combine the cherries, sugar, cornstarch, lemon juice, vanilla extract, and almond extract if using. Toss to coat the cherries evenly. Set aside.
3. **Assemble the Pie:**
    1. Preheat your oven to 425°F (220°C).
    2. Roll out one disk of dough to fit a 9-inch pie dish. Carefully transfer it to the dish, pressing it into the bottom and up the sides.
    3. Pour the cherry filling into the crust, and dot with the pieces of butter.
    4. Roll out the second disk of dough and place it over the filling. Trim any excess dough and crimp the edges to seal. Cut slits in the top crust to allow steam to escape, or create a lattice pattern if desired.

    5. Brush the top crust with the beaten egg and sprinkle with sugar.
4. **Bake the Pie:**
    1. Place the pie on a baking sheet and bake in the preheated oven for 45-50 minutes, or until the crust is golden and the filling is bubbly.
    2. If the edges of the crust start to brown too quickly, cover them with aluminum foil.
5. **Cool and Serve:**
    1. Allow the pie to cool on a wire rack for at least 2 hours before serving to let the filling set.

Pumpkin Pie

Ingredients:

- **For the Pie Crust:**
    - 1 ½ cups all-purpose flour
    - ½ tsp salt
    - ¼ cup granulated sugar
    - ½ cup (1 stick) unsalted butter, chilled and cut into small cubes
    - 2-4 tbsp ice water
- **For the Filling:**
    - 1 can (15 oz) pumpkin puree
    - ¾ cup granulated sugar
    - 1 tsp ground cinnamon
    - ½ tsp ground ginger
    - ¼ tsp ground nutmeg
    - ¼ tsp salt
    - 3 large eggs
    - 1 cup heavy cream
    - ½ cup whole milk
- **For Assembly:**
    - Whipped cream (optional, for serving)

Instructions:

1. **Prepare the Pie Crust:**
    1. In a large bowl, whisk together the flour, salt, and sugar.
    2. Add the chilled butter and use a pastry cutter or your fingers to work it into the flour until the mixture resembles coarse crumbs.
    3. Gradually add the ice water, one tablespoon at a time, mixing until the dough just comes together. Do not overwork.
    4. Flatten the dough into a disk, wrap in plastic wrap, and chill in the refrigerator for at least 30 minutes.
2. **Prepare the Filling:**
    1. In a large bowl, whisk together the pumpkin puree, sugar, cinnamon, ginger, nutmeg, and salt.
    2. Add the eggs, one at a time, mixing well after each addition.
    3. Gradually add the heavy cream and milk, whisking until smooth.

3. **Assemble the Pie:**
    1. Preheat your oven to 425°F (220°C).
    2. Roll out the chilled dough to fit a 9-inch pie dish. Carefully transfer it to the dish, pressing it into the bottom and up the sides.
    3. Pour the pumpkin filling into the crust.
4. **Bake the Pie:**
    1. Bake in the preheated oven for 15 minutes.
    2. Reduce the temperature to 350°F (175°C) and continue to bake for 35-40 minutes, or until the filling is set and a knife inserted into the center comes out clean.
    3. If the crust starts to over-brown, cover the edges with aluminum foil.
5. **Cool and Serve:**
    1. Allow the pie to cool completely on a wire rack before serving. Serve with whipped cream if desired.

Pecan Pie

Ingredients:

- **For the Pie Crust:**
    - 1 ½ cups all-purpose flour
    - ¼ tsp salt
    - ¼ cup granulated sugar
    - ½ cup (1 stick) unsalted butter, chilled and cut into small cubes
    - 2-4 tbsp ice water
- **For the Filling:**
    - 1 cup light corn syrup
    - 1 cup packed brown sugar
    - ¼ cup unsalted butter, melted
    - 4 large eggs
    - 1 tsp vanilla extract
    - 2 cups pecan halves
- **For Assembly:**
    - Whipped cream (optional, for serving)

Instructions:

1. **Prepare the Pie Crust:**
    1. In a large bowl, whisk together the flour, salt, and sugar.
    2. Add the chilled butter and use a pastry cutter or your fingers to work it into the flour until the mixture resembles coarse crumbs.
    3. Gradually add the ice water, one tablespoon at a time, mixing until the dough just comes together. Do not overwork.
    4. Flatten the dough into a disk, wrap in plastic wrap, and chill in the refrigerator for at least 30 minutes.
2. **Prepare the Filling:**
    1. In a large bowl, whisk together the corn syrup, brown sugar, melted butter, eggs, and vanilla extract until well combined.
    2. Stir in the pecan halves.
3. **Assemble the Pie:**
    1. Preheat your oven to 350°F (175°C).
    2. Roll out the chilled dough to fit a 9-inch pie dish. Carefully transfer it to the dish, pressing it into the bottom and up the sides.

    3. Pour the pecan filling into the crust.
 4. **Bake the Pie:**
    1. Bake in the preheated oven for 50-60 minutes, or until the filling is set and the crust is golden brown.
    2. If the crust edges begin to over-brown, cover them with aluminum foil.
 5. **Cool and Serve:**
    1. Allow the pie to cool completely on a wire rack before serving. Serve with whipped cream if desired.

Blueberry Pie

Ingredients:

- **For the Pie Crust:**
    - 2 ½ cups all-purpose flour
    - 1 tsp salt
    - 1 tsp sugar
    - 1 cup (2 sticks) unsalted butter, chilled and cut into small cubes
    - 6-8 tbsp ice water
- **For the Filling:**
    - 4 cups fresh or frozen blueberries
    - ¾ cup granulated sugar
    - ¼ cup cornstarch
    - 1 tsp lemon juice
    - 1 tsp vanilla extract
    - ¼ tsp ground cinnamon
    - 1 tbsp unsalted butter, cut into small pieces
- **For Assembly:**
    - 1 egg, beaten (for egg wash)
    - 1 tbsp sugar (for sprinkling)

Instructions:

1. **Prepare the Pie Crust:**
    1. In a large bowl, whisk together the flour, salt, and sugar.
    2. Add the chilled butter and use a pastry cutter or your fingers to work it into the flour until the mixture resembles coarse crumbs.
    3. Gradually add the ice water, one tablespoon at a time, mixing until the dough just comes together. Do not overwork.

        4. Divide the dough into two equal portions, flatten each into a disk, and wrap in plastic wrap. Chill in the refrigerator for at least 1 hour.
2. **Prepare the Filling:**
    1. In a large bowl, combine the blueberries, sugar, cornstarch, lemon juice, vanilla extract, and cinnamon. Toss to coat the blueberries evenly. Set aside.
3. **Assemble the Pie:**
    1. Preheat your oven to 425°F (220°C).
    2. On a lightly floured surface, roll out one disk of dough to fit a 9-inch pie dish. Carefully transfer it to the dish, pressing it into the bottom and up the sides.
    3. Pour the blueberry filling into the crust and dot with the pieces of butter.
    4. Roll out the second disk of dough and place it over the filling. Trim any excess dough and crimp the edges to seal. You can also cut the dough into strips and create a lattice top if you prefer.
    5. Brush the top crust with the beaten egg and sprinkle with sugar.
4. **Bake the Pie:**
    1. Place the pie on a baking sheet and bake in the preheated oven for 45-50 minutes, or until the crust is golden brown and the filling is bubbly.
    2. If the edges of the crust start to brown too quickly, cover them with aluminum foil.
5. **Cool and Serve:**
    1. Allow the pie to cool on a wire rack for at least 2 hours before serving to let the filling set.

Peach Pie

Ingredients:

- **For the Pie Crust:**
    - 2 ½ cups all-purpose flour
    - 1 tsp salt
    - 1 tsp sugar
    - 1 cup (2 sticks) unsalted butter, chilled and cut into small cubes
    - 6-8 tbsp ice water
- **For the Filling:**
    - 6 cups peeled and sliced fresh peaches (or frozen, thawed, and drained)
    - ¾ cup granulated sugar
    - ¼ cup packed brown sugar
    - ¼ cup cornstarch
    - 1 tsp lemon juice
    - 1 tsp vanilla extract
    - ¼ tsp ground cinnamon
    - 1 tbsp unsalted butter, cut into small pieces
- **For Assembly:**
    - 1 egg, beaten (for egg wash)
    - 1 tbsp sugar (for sprinkling)

Instructions:

1. **Prepare the Pie Crust:**
    1. Follow the same instructions as for the blueberry pie crust.
2. **Prepare the Filling:**
    1. In a large bowl, combine the peaches, granulated sugar, brown sugar, cornstarch, lemon juice, vanilla extract, and cinnamon. Toss to coat the peaches evenly. Set aside.
3. **Assemble the Pie:**
    1. Preheat your oven to 425°F (220°C).
    2. Roll out one disk of dough to fit a 9-inch pie dish. Carefully transfer it to the dish, pressing it into the bottom and up the sides.
    3. Pour the peach filling into the crust and dot with the pieces of butter.

4. Roll out the second disk of dough and place it over the filling. Trim any excess dough and crimp the edges to seal. Cut slits in the top crust for steam to escape, or create a lattice pattern if preferred.
5. Brush the top crust with the beaten egg and sprinkle with sugar.

4. **Bake the Pie:**
    1. Place the pie on a baking sheet and bake in the preheated oven for 45-50 minutes, or until the crust is golden and the filling is bubbling.
    2. If the edges of the crust start to brown too quickly, cover them with aluminum foil.
5. **Cool and Serve:**
    1. Allow the pie to cool on a wire rack for at least 2 hours before serving to let the filling set.

Lemon Meringue Pie

Ingredients:

- **For the Pie Crust:**
    - 1 ½ cups graham cracker crumbs
    - ¼ cup granulated sugar
    - 6 tbsp unsalted butter, melted
- **For the Lemon Filling:**
    - 1 cup granulated sugar
    - 2 tbsp cornstarch
    - ¼ tsp salt
    - 1 ½ cups water
    - 3 large egg yolks, lightly beaten
    - ¼ cup fresh lemon juice (about 2 lemons)
    - 2 tbsp unsalted butter
    - 1 tsp lemon zest (optional)
- **For the Meringue:**
    - 3 large egg whites
    - ¼ tsp cream of tartar
    - ¼ cup granulated sugar
    - ¼ tsp vanilla extract

Instructions:

1. **Prepare the Pie Crust:**
    1. Preheat your oven to 350°F (175°C).
    2. In a medium bowl, combine the graham cracker crumbs, sugar, and melted butter. Mix until well combined.
    3. Press the mixture into the bottom and up the sides of a 9-inch pie dish.
    4. Bake for 8-10 minutes, then let cool completely.
2. **Prepare the Lemon Filling:**
    1. In a medium saucepan, whisk together the sugar, cornstarch, and salt.
    2. Gradually whisk in the water and cook over medium heat, stirring constantly, until the mixture thickens and starts to boil.
    3. Reduce the heat to low and whisk a small amount of the hot mixture into the egg yolks to temper them. Gradually whisk the egg yolks back into the saucepan.

4. Cook for an additional 2 minutes, then remove from heat and stir in the lemon juice, butter, and lemon zest if using.
   5. Pour the lemon filling into the cooled pie crust.
3. **Prepare the Meringue:**
   1. In a large, clean bowl, beat the egg whites with cream of tartar until soft peaks form.
   2. Gradually add the sugar, continuing to beat until stiff peaks form. Beat in the vanilla extract.
   3. Spread the meringue over the lemon filling, making sure to seal the edges well.
4. **Bake the Pie:**
   1. Bake in the preheated oven for 10-12 minutes, or until the meringue is golden brown.
   2. Let the pie cool completely on a wire rack before serving.

Key Lime Pie

Ingredients:

- **For the Pie Crust:**
    - 1 ½ cups graham cracker crumbs
    - ¼ cup granulated sugar
    - 6 tbsp unsalted butter, melted
- **For the Filling:**
    - 1 can (14 oz) sweetened condensed milk
    - ½ cup fresh lime juice (about 4 limes)
    - 1 cup sour cream
    - 1 tsp lime zest (optional)
- **For Assembly:**
    - Whipped cream (optional, for topping)
    - Lime slices or zest (for garnish)

Instructions:

1. **Prepare the Pie Crust:**
    1. Preheat your oven to 350°F (175°C).
    2. In a medium bowl, combine the graham cracker crumbs, sugar, and melted butter. Mix until well combined.
    3. Press the mixture into the bottom and up the sides of a 9-inch pie dish.
    4. Bake for 8-10 minutes, then let cool completely.
2. **Prepare the Filling:**
    1. In a medium bowl, whisk together the sweetened condensed milk, lime juice, sour cream, and lime zest if using.
    2. Pour the filling into the cooled pie crust.
3. **Bake the Pie:**
    1. Bake in the preheated oven for 10-12 minutes, or until the filling is set but still slightly jiggly in the center.
    2. Let the pie cool to room temperature, then refrigerate for at least 3 hours before serving.
4. **Serve:**
    1. Top with whipped cream and garnish with lime slices or zest if desired.

Chocolate Cream Pie

Ingredients:

- **For the Pie Crust:**
    - 1 ½ cups graham cracker crumbs
    - ¼ cup granulated sugar
    - 6 tbsp unsalted butter, melted
- **For the Chocolate Filling:**
    - 1 cup whole milk
    - 1 cup heavy cream
    - ½ cup granulated sugar
    - ¼ cup unsweetened cocoa powder
    - 3 large egg yolks
    - 2 tbsp cornstarch
    - 1 tsp vanilla extract
    - 4 oz bittersweet or semi-sweet chocolate, finely chopped
- **For Topping:**
    - 1 cup heavy cream
    - 2 tbsp granulated sugar
    - 1 tsp vanilla extract
    - Chocolate shavings or cocoa powder (optional)

Instructions:

1. **Prepare the Pie Crust:**
    1. Preheat your oven to 350°F (175°C).
    2. In a medium bowl, combine the graham cracker crumbs, sugar, and melted butter. Mix until well combined.
    3. Press the mixture into the bottom and up the sides of a 9-inch pie dish.
    4. Bake for 8-10 minutes, then let cool completely.
2. **Prepare the Chocolate Filling:**
    1. In a medium saucepan, heat the milk and cream over medium heat until just below boiling.
    2. In a separate bowl, whisk together the sugar, cocoa powder, egg yolks, and cornstarch until smooth.
    3. Gradually whisk the hot milk mixture into the egg yolk mixture to temper, then return the mixture to the saucepan.

4. Cook over medium heat, whisking constantly, until the mixture thickens and begins to boil.
   5. Remove from heat and stir in the chopped chocolate and vanilla extract until smooth.
   6. Pour the filling into the cooled pie crust.
3. **Prepare the Topping:**
   1. In a medium bowl, beat the heavy cream, sugar, and vanilla extract until stiff peaks form.
   2. Spread the whipped cream over the chocolate filling.
   3. Garnish with chocolate shavings or a dusting of cocoa powder if desired.
4. **Chill and Serve:**
   1. Refrigerate the pie for at least 3 hours before serving to allow the filling to set.

Banana Cream Pie

Ingredients:

- **For the Pie Crust:**
    - 1 ½ cups graham cracker crumbs
    - ¼ cup granulated sugar
    - 6 tbsp unsalted butter, melted
- **For the Filling:**
    - 1 cup whole milk
    - 1 cup heavy cream
    - ¾ cup granulated sugar
    - ¼ cup cornstarch
    - ¼ tsp salt
    - 3 large egg yolks
    - 1 tsp vanilla extract
    - 3-4 ripe bananas, sliced
- **For Topping:**
    - 1 cup heavy cream
    - 2 tbsp granulated sugar
    - 1 tsp vanilla extract
    - Extra banana slices (for garnish)

Instructions:

1. **Prepare the Pie Crust:**
    1. Preheat your oven to 350°F (175°C).
    2. In a medium bowl, combine the graham cracker crumbs, sugar, and melted butter. Mix until well combined.
    3. Press the mixture into the bottom and up the sides of a 9-inch pie dish.
    4. Bake for 8-10 minutes, then let cool completely.
2. **Prepare the Filling:**
    1. In a medium saucepan, whisk together the milk, cream, sugar, cornstarch, and salt.
    2. Cook over medium heat, whisking constantly, until the mixture thickens and begins to boil.

3. Remove from heat and whisk a small amount of the hot mixture into the egg yolks to temper them. Gradually whisk the egg yolks back into the saucepan.
4. Cook for an additional 2 minutes, then remove from heat and stir in the vanilla extract.
5. Let the mixture cool slightly before layering sliced bananas in the cooled pie crust and pouring the filling over them.

3. **Prepare the Topping:**
   1. In a medium bowl, beat the heavy cream, sugar, and vanilla extract until stiff peaks form.
   2. Spread the whipped cream over the filling.
   3. Garnish with extra banana slices.

4. **Chill and Serve:**
   1. Refrigerate the pie for at least 3 hours before serving to allow the filling to set.

Sweet Potato Pie

Ingredients:

- **For the Pie Crust:**
    - 1 ½ cups all-purpose flour
    - ½ tsp salt
    - ¼ cup granulated sugar
    - ½ cup (1 stick) unsalted butter, chilled and cut into small cubes
    - 2-4 tbsp ice water
- **For the Filling:**
    - 2 cups mashed cooked sweet potatoes (about 2 medium sweet potatoes)
    - ¾ cup granulated sugar
    - ½ cup packed brown sugar
    - 1 tsp ground cinnamon
    - ½ tsp ground ginger
    - ¼ tsp ground nutmeg
    - ¼ tsp salt
    - 3 large eggs
    - 1 cup evaporated milk
    - 2 tbsp unsalted butter, melted
- **For Assembly:**
    - Whipped cream (optional, for topping)

Instructions:

1. **Prepare the Pie Crust:**
    1. In a large bowl, whisk together the flour, salt, and sugar.
    2. Add the chilled butter and use a pastry cutter or your fingers to work it into the flour until the mixture resembles coarse crumbs.
    3. Gradually add the ice water, one tablespoon at a time, mixing until the dough just comes together. Do not overwork.
    4. Flatten the dough into a disk, wrap in plastic wrap, and chill in the refrigerator for at least 30 minutes.
2. **Prepare the Filling:**
    1. Preheat your oven to 350°F (175°C).
    2. In a large bowl, mix the mashed sweet potatoes, granulated sugar, brown sugar, cinnamon, ginger, nutmeg, and salt until well combined.

3. Add the eggs, one at a time, mixing well after each addition.
4. Gradually add the evaporated milk and melted butter, mixing until smooth.

3. **Assemble the Pie:**
    1. Roll out the chilled dough and fit it into a 9-inch pie dish.
    2. Pour the sweet potato filling into the crust.
4. **Bake the Pie:**
    1. Bake in the preheated oven for 50-60 minutes, or until the filling is set and the crust is golden brown.
    2. If the crust edges start to over-brown, cover them with aluminum foil.
5. **Serve:**
    1. Allow the pie to cool before serving. Top with whipped cream if desired.

Coconut Cream Pie

Ingredients:

- **For the Pie Crust:**
    - 1 ½ cups graham cracker crumbs
    - ¼ cup granulated sugar
    - 6 tbsp unsalted butter, melted
- **For the Coconut Filling:**
    - 1 cup whole milk
    - 1 cup heavy cream
    - ¾ cup granulated sugar
    - ¼ cup cornstarch
    - ¼ tsp salt
    - 3 large egg yolks
    - 1 cup sweetened shredded coconut
    - 1 tsp vanilla extract
- **For Topping:**
    - 1 cup heavy cream
    - 2 tbsp granulated sugar
    - 1 tsp vanilla extract
    - Toasted shredded coconut (for garnish)

Instructions:

1. **Prepare the Pie Crust:**
    1. Preheat your oven to 350°F (175°C).
    2. In a medium bowl, combine the graham cracker crumbs, sugar, and melted butter. Mix until well combined.
    3. Press the mixture into the bottom and up the sides of a 9-inch pie dish.
    4. Bake for 8-10 minutes, then let cool completely.
2. **Prepare the Coconut Filling:**
    1. In a medium saucepan, whisk together the milk, cream, sugar, cornstarch, and salt.
    2. Cook over medium heat, whisking constantly, until the mixture thickens and begins to boil.

3. Remove from heat and whisk a small amount of the hot mixture into the egg yolks to temper them. Gradually whisk the egg yolks back into the saucepan.
4. Cook for an additional 2 minutes, then remove from heat and stir in the shredded coconut and vanilla extract.
5. Let the filling cool slightly before pouring it into the cooled pie crust.

3. **Prepare the Topping:**
    1. In a medium bowl, beat the heavy cream, sugar, and vanilla extract until stiff peaks form.
    2. Spread the whipped cream over the coconut filling.
    3. Garnish with toasted shredded coconut.
4. **Chill and Serve:**
    1. Refrigerate the pie for at least 3 hours before serving to allow the filling to set.

Strawberry Rhubarb Pie

Ingredients:

- **For the Pie Crust:**
    - 2 ½ cups all-purpose flour
    - 1 tsp salt
    - 1 tsp sugar
    - 1 cup (2 sticks) unsalted butter, chilled and cut into small cubes
    - 6-8 tbsp ice water
- **For the Filling:**
    - 2 cups fresh strawberries, hulled and sliced
    - 2 cups fresh rhubarb, chopped
    - 1 cup granulated sugar
    - ¼ cup cornstarch
    - 1 tsp lemon juice
    - 1 tsp vanilla extract
    - ¼ tsp ground cinnamon
    - 1 egg, beaten (for egg wash)
    - 1 tbsp sugar (for sprinkling)

Instructions:

1. **Prepare the Pie Crust:**
    1. In a large bowl, whisk together the flour, salt, and sugar.
    2. Add the chilled butter and use a pastry cutter or your fingers to work it into the flour until the mixture resembles coarse crumbs.
    3. Gradually add the ice water, one tablespoon at a time, mixing until the dough just comes together. Do not overwork.
    4. Divide the dough into two equal portions, flatten each into a disk, and wrap in plastic wrap. Chill in the refrigerator for at least 1 hour.
2. **Prepare the Filling:**
    1. In a large bowl, combine the strawberries, rhubarb, sugar, cornstarch, lemon juice, vanilla extract, and cinnamon. Toss to coat the fruit evenly. Set aside.
3. **Assemble the Pie:**
    1. Preheat your oven to 425°F (220°C).

2. On a lightly floured surface, roll out one disk of dough to fit a 9-inch pie dish. Carefully transfer it to the dish, pressing it into the bottom and up the sides.
3. Pour the strawberry rhubarb filling into the crust.
4. Roll out the second disk of dough and place it over the filling. Trim any excess dough and crimp the edges to seal. Cut slits in the top crust for steam to escape, or create a lattice pattern if preferred.
5. Brush the top crust with the beaten egg and sprinkle with sugar.

4. **Bake the Pie:**
    1. Place the pie on a baking sheet and bake in the preheated oven for 45-50 minutes, or until the crust is golden and the filling is bubbly.
    2. If the edges of the crust start to over-brown, cover them with aluminum foil.
5. **Cool and Serve:**
    1. Allow the pie to cool on a wire rack for at least 2 hours before serving to let the filling set.

Maple Pecan Pie

Ingredients:

- **For the Pie Crust:**
    - 1 ½ cups all-purpose flour
    - ½ tsp salt
    - 2 tbsp granulated sugar
    - ½ cup (1 stick) unsalted butter, chilled and cut into small cubes
    - 2-4 tbsp ice water
- **For the Filling:**
    - 1 cup pure maple syrup
    - ½ cup packed brown sugar
    - ¼ cup unsalted butter, melted
    - 3 large eggs
    - 1 tsp vanilla extract
    - 1 ½ cups pecan halves

Instructions:

1. **Prepare the Pie Crust:**
    1. In a large bowl, whisk together the flour, salt, and sugar.
    2. Add the chilled butter and use a pastry cutter or your fingers to work it into the flour until the mixture resembles coarse crumbs.
    3. Gradually add the ice water, one tablespoon at a time, mixing until the dough just comes together. Do not overwork.
    4. Flatten the dough into a disk, wrap in plastic wrap, and chill in the refrigerator for at least 30 minutes.
2. **Prepare the Filling:**
    1. Preheat your oven to 350°F (175°C).
    2. In a large bowl, whisk together the maple syrup, brown sugar, melted butter, eggs, and vanilla extract until smooth.
    3. Stir in the pecan halves.
3. **Assemble the Pie:**
    1. Roll out the chilled dough to fit a 9-inch pie dish. Carefully transfer it to the dish, pressing it into the bottom and up the sides.
    2. Pour the pecan filling into the crust.
4. **Bake the Pie:**

1. Bake in the preheated oven for 50-60 minutes, or until the filling is set and the crust is golden brown.
2. If the crust edges start to over-brown, cover them with aluminum foil.

5. **Cool and Serve:**
   1. Allow the pie to cool completely on a wire rack before serving. Serve with whipped cream if desired.

Raspberry Pie

Ingredients:

- **For the Pie Crust:**
    - 2 ½ cups all-purpose flour
    - 1 tsp salt
    - 1 tsp sugar
    - 1 cup (2 sticks) unsalted butter, chilled and cut into small cubes
    - 6-8 tbsp ice water
- **For the Filling:**
    - 4 cups fresh or frozen raspberries
    - ¾ cup granulated sugar
    - ¼ cup cornstarch
    - 1 tsp lemon juice
    - 1 tsp vanilla extract
    - ¼ tsp ground cinnamon
    - 1 egg, beaten (for egg wash)
    - 1 tbsp sugar (for sprinkling)

Instructions:

1. **Prepare the Pie Crust:**
    1. In a large bowl, whisk together the flour, salt, and sugar.
    2. Add the chilled butter and use a pastry cutter or your fingers to work it into the flour until the mixture resembles coarse crumbs.
    3. Gradually add the ice water, one tablespoon at a time, mixing until the dough just comes together. Do not overwork.
    4. Divide the dough into two equal portions, flatten each into a disk, and wrap in plastic wrap. Chill in the refrigerator for at least 1 hour.
2. **Prepare the Filling:**
    1. In a large bowl, combine the raspberries, sugar, cornstarch, lemon juice, vanilla extract, and cinnamon. Toss to coat the raspberries evenly. Set aside.
3. **Assemble the Pie:**
    1. Preheat your oven to 425°F (220°C).

2. On a lightly floured surface, roll out one disk of dough to fit a 9-inch pie dish. Carefully transfer it to the dish, pressing it into the bottom and up the sides.
3. Pour the raspberry filling into the crust.
4. Roll out the second disk of dough and place it over the filling. Trim any excess dough and crimp the edges to seal. Cut slits in the top crust for steam to escape, or create a lattice pattern if preferred.
5. Brush the top crust with the beaten egg and sprinkle with sugar.

4. **Bake the Pie:**
    1. Place the pie on a baking sheet and bake in the preheated oven for 45-50 minutes, or until the crust is golden and the filling is bubbly.
    2. If the edges of the crust start to over-brown, cover them with aluminum foil.
5. **Cool and Serve:**
    1. Allow the pie to cool on a wire rack for at least 2 hours before serving to let the filling set.

Buttermilk Pie

Ingredients:

- **For the Pie Crust:**
    - 1 ½ cups all-purpose flour
    - ½ tsp salt
    - 2 tbsp granulated sugar
    - ½ cup (1 stick) unsalted butter, chilled and cut into small cubes
    - 2-4 tbsp ice water
- **For the Filling:**
    - 1 ½ cups granulated sugar
    - ¼ cup all-purpose flour
    - ¼ tsp salt
    - 3 large eggs
    - 1 cup buttermilk
    - 1 tsp vanilla extract
    - 2 tbsp unsalted butter, melted
    - ¼ tsp ground nutmeg (optional)

Instructions:

1. **Prepare the Pie Crust:**
    1. In a large bowl, whisk together the flour, salt, and sugar.
    2. Add the chilled butter and use a pastry cutter or your fingers to work it into the flour until the mixture resembles coarse crumbs.
    3. Gradually add the ice water, one tablespoon at a time, mixing until the dough just comes together. Do not overwork.
    4. Flatten the dough into a disk, wrap in plastic wrap, and chill in the refrigerator for at least 30 minutes.
2. **Prepare the Filling:**
    1. Preheat your oven to 350°F (175°C).
    2. In a large bowl, whisk together the sugar, flour, and salt.
    3. Add the eggs, one at a time, mixing well after each addition.
    4. Gradually add the buttermilk, vanilla extract, and melted butter, mixing until smooth.
    5. Pour the filling into the chilled pie crust and sprinkle with nutmeg if using.
3. **Bake the Pie:**

1. Bake in the preheated oven for 50-60 minutes, or until the filling is set and the top is golden brown.
2. If the edges of the crust start to over-brown, cover them with aluminum foil.

4. **Cool and Serve:**
    1. Allow the pie to cool completely on a wire rack before serving. The pie will firm up as it cools.

Mincemeat Pie

Ingredients:

- **For the Pie Crust:**
    - 2 ½ cups all-purpose flour
    - 1 tsp salt
    - 1 tsp sugar
    - 1 cup (2 sticks) unsalted butter, chilled and cut into small cubes
    - 6-8 tbsp ice water
- **For the Mincemeat Filling:**
    - 1 jar (about 24 oz) prepared mincemeat
    - 1 small apple, peeled, cored, and finely diced
    - ¼ cup chopped suet (or substitute with butter)
    - ½ cup dark brown sugar
    - 1 tsp ground cinnamon
    - ¼ tsp ground cloves
    - ¼ tsp ground nutmeg
    - 2 tbsp brandy (optional)

Instructions:

1. **Prepare the Pie Crust:**
    1. In a large bowl, whisk together the flour, salt, and sugar.
    2. Add the chilled butter and use a pastry cutter or your fingers to work it into the flour until the mixture resembles coarse crumbs.
    3. Gradually add the ice water, one tablespoon at a time, mixing until the dough just comes together. Do not overwork.
    4. Divide the dough into two equal portions, flatten each into a disk, and wrap in plastic wrap. Chill in the refrigerator for at least 1 hour.
2. **Prepare the Mincemeat Filling:**
    1. In a large bowl, mix together the mincemeat, diced apple, chopped suet, brown sugar, cinnamon, cloves, nutmeg, and brandy if using.
3. **Assemble the Pie:**
    1. Preheat your oven to 425°F (220°C).
    2. On a lightly floured surface, roll out one disk of dough to fit a 9-inch pie dish. Carefully transfer it to the dish, pressing it into the bottom and up the sides.

3. Pour the mincemeat filling into the crust.
4. Roll out the second disk of dough and place it over the filling. Trim any excess dough and crimp the edges to seal. Cut slits in the top crust for steam to escape or use a decorative lattice pattern.
5. Brush the top crust with milk or an egg wash and sprinkle with a little sugar.

4. **Bake the Pie:**
    1. Bake in the preheated oven for 45-50 minutes, or until the crust is golden brown and the filling is bubbling.
    2. If the crust edges start to over-brown, cover them with aluminum foil.
5. **Cool and Serve:**
    1. Allow the pie to cool on a wire rack before serving. The filling will firm up as it cools.

Shoofly Pie

Ingredients:

- **For the Pie Crust:**
    - 1 ½ cups all-purpose flour
    - ½ tsp salt
    - 2 tbsp granulated sugar
    - ½ cup (1 stick) unsalted butter, chilled and cut into small cubes
    - 2-4 tbsp ice water
- **For the Filling:**
    - 1 cup dark brown sugar
    - ½ cup all-purpose flour
    - ½ tsp baking powder
    - ½ tsp baking soda
    - ¼ cup unsalted butter, melted
    - ¾ cup boiling water
    - 1 egg, beaten
    - 1 tbsp molasses
- **For the Crumb Topping:**
    - 1 cup all-purpose flour
    - ½ cup granulated sugar
    - ¼ cup unsalted butter, chilled and cut into small cubes

Instructions:

1. **Prepare the Pie Crust:**
    1. In a large bowl, whisk together the flour, salt, and sugar.
    2. Add the chilled butter and use a pastry cutter or your fingers to work it into the flour until the mixture resembles coarse crumbs.
    3. Gradually add the ice water, one tablespoon at a time, mixing until the dough just comes together. Do not overwork.
    4. Flatten the dough into a disk, wrap in plastic wrap, and chill in the refrigerator for at least 30 minutes.
2. **Prepare the Filling:**
    1. Preheat your oven to 375°F (190°C).
    2. In a large bowl, whisk together the brown sugar, flour, baking powder, and baking soda.

3. Add the melted butter, boiling water, beaten egg, and molasses. Stir until well combined.
3. **Prepare the Crumb Topping:**
    1. In a separate bowl, combine the flour, sugar, and chilled butter. Use a pastry cutter or your fingers to mix until the mixture resembles coarse crumbs.
4. **Assemble the Pie:**
    1. Roll out the chilled dough to fit a 9-inch pie dish. Carefully transfer it to the dish, pressing it into the bottom and up the sides.
    2. Pour the filling into the crust.
    3. Sprinkle the crumb topping evenly over the filling.
5. **Bake the Pie:**
    1. Bake in the preheated oven for 45-50 minutes, or until the filling is set and the topping is golden brown.
    2. If the topping starts to over-brown, cover it with aluminum foil.
6. **Cool and Serve:**
    1. Allow the pie to cool completely on a wire rack before serving.

Chicken Pot Pie

Ingredients:

- **For the Pie Crust:**
    - 2 ½ cups all-purpose flour
    - 1 tsp salt
    - 1 tsp sugar
    - 1 cup (2 sticks) unsalted butter, chilled and cut into small cubes
    - 6-8 tbsp ice water
- **For the Filling:**
    - 2 cups cooked chicken, diced
    - 1 cup carrots, diced
    - 1 cup peas
    - 1 cup potatoes, diced
    - 1 small onion, finely chopped
    - ¼ cup unsalted butter
    - ¼ cup all-purpose flour
    - 1 cup chicken broth
    - 1 cup milk
    - 1 tsp dried thyme
    - 1 tsp dried rosemary
    - Salt and pepper to taste
    - 1 egg, beaten (for egg wash)

Instructions:

1. **Prepare the Pie Crust:**
    1. In a large bowl, whisk together the flour, salt, and sugar.
    2. Add the chilled butter and use a pastry cutter or your fingers to work it into the flour until the mixture resembles coarse crumbs.
    3. Gradually add the ice water, one tablespoon at a time, mixing until the dough just comes together. Do not overwork.
    4. Divide the dough into two equal portions, flatten each into a disk, and wrap in plastic wrap. Chill in the refrigerator for at least 1 hour.
2. **Prepare the Filling:**
    1. Preheat your oven to 425°F (220°C).

2. In a large skillet, melt the butter over medium heat. Add the onion and cook until softened.
   3. Stir in the flour and cook for 1-2 minutes to form a roux.
   4. Gradually whisk in the chicken broth and milk, and cook until the mixture thickens.
   5. Add the chicken, carrots, peas, potatoes, thyme, rosemary, salt, and pepper. Stir to combine and heat through.
3. **Assemble the Pie:**
   1. Roll out one disk of dough to fit a 9-inch pie dish. Carefully transfer it to the dish, pressing it into the bottom and up the sides.
   2. Pour the filling into the crust.
   3. Roll out the second disk of dough and place it over the filling. Trim any excess dough and crimp the edges to seal. Cut slits in the top crust for steam to escape.
   4. Brush the top crust with the beaten egg.
4. **Bake the Pie:**
   1. Bake in the preheated oven for 45-50 minutes, or until the crust is golden and the filling is bubbly.
   2. If the crust edges start to over-brown, cover them with aluminum foil.
5. **Cool and Serve:**
   1. Allow the pie to cool for a few minutes before serving.

Beef Pot Pie

Ingredients:

- **For the Pie Crust:**
    - 2 ½ cups all-purpose flour
    - 1 tsp salt
    - 1 tsp sugar
    - 1 cup (2 sticks) unsalted butter, chilled and cut into small cubes
    - 6-8 tbsp ice water
- **For the Filling:**
    - 2 cups cooked beef, diced (such as leftover roast beef or beef stew meat)
    - 1 cup carrots, diced
    - 1 cup peas
    - 1 cup potatoes, diced
    - 1 small onion, finely chopped
    - 2 cloves garlic, minced
    - ¼ cup unsalted butter
    - ¼ cup all-purpose flour
    - 1 cup beef broth
    - 1 cup milk
    - 1 tsp dried thyme
    - 1 tsp dried rosemary
    - Salt and pepper to taste
    - 1 egg, beaten (for egg wash)

Instructions:

1. **Prepare the Pie Crust:**
    1. In a large bowl, whisk together the flour, salt, and sugar.
    2. Add the chilled butter and use a pastry cutter or your fingers to work it into the flour until the mixture resembles coarse crumbs.
    3. Gradually add the ice water, one tablespoon at a time, mixing until the dough just comes together. Do not overwork.
    4. Divide the dough into two equal portions, flatten each into a disk, and wrap in plastic wrap. Chill in the refrigerator for at least 1 hour.
2. **Prepare the Filling:**
    1. Preheat your oven to 425°F (220°C).

2. In a large skillet, melt the butter over medium heat. Add the onion and garlic and cook until softened.
   3. Stir in the flour and cook for 1-2 minutes to form a roux.
   4. Gradually whisk in the beef broth and milk, and cook until the mixture thickens.
   5. Add the beef, carrots, peas, potatoes, thyme, rosemary, salt, and pepper. Stir to combine and heat through.
3. **Assemble the Pie:**
   1. Roll out one disk of dough to fit a 9-inch pie dish. Carefully transfer it to the dish, pressing it into the bottom and up the sides.
   2. Pour the filling into the crust.
   3. Roll out the second disk of dough and place it over the filling. Trim any excess dough and crimp the edges to seal. Cut slits in the top crust for steam to escape.
   4. Brush the top crust with the beaten egg.
4. **Bake the Pie:**
   1. Bake in the preheated oven for 45-50 minutes, or until the crust is golden and the filling is bubbly.
   2. If the crust edges start to over-brown, cover them with aluminum foil.
5. **Cool and Serve:**
   1. Allow the pie to cool for a few minutes before serving.

Spinach and Feta Pie

Ingredients:

- **For the Pie Crust:**
    - 1 ½ cups all-purpose flour
    - ½ tsp salt
    - 2 tbsp granulated sugar
    - ½ cup (1 stick) unsalted butter, chilled and cut into small cubes
    - 2-4 tbsp ice water
- **For the Filling:**
    - 1 tbsp olive oil
    - 1 small onion, finely chopped
    - 2 cloves garlic, minced
    - 4 cups fresh spinach, chopped
    - ½ cup crumbled feta cheese
    - 3 large eggs
    - 1 cup heavy cream
    - ¼ tsp ground nutmeg
    - Salt and pepper to taste

Instructions:

1. **Prepare the Pie Crust:**
    1. In a large bowl, whisk together the flour, salt, and sugar.
    2. Add the chilled butter and use a pastry cutter or your fingers to work it into the flour until the mixture resembles coarse crumbs.
    3. Gradually add the ice water, one tablespoon at a time, mixing until the dough just comes together. Do not overwork.
    4. Flatten the dough into a disk, wrap in plastic wrap, and chill in the refrigerator for at least 30 minutes.
2. **Prepare the Filling:**
    1. Preheat your oven to 375°F (190°C).
    2. Heat the olive oil in a skillet over medium heat. Add the onion and garlic, and sauté until softened.
    3. Add the spinach and cook until wilted. Remove from heat and let cool.
    4. In a large bowl, whisk together the eggs, heavy cream, nutmeg, salt, and pepper.

5. Stir in the spinach mixture and crumbled feta cheese.
3. **Assemble the Pie:**
   1. Roll out the chilled dough to fit a 9-inch pie dish. Carefully transfer it to the dish, pressing it into the bottom and up the sides.
   2. Pour the filling into the crust.
4. **Bake the Pie:**
   1. Bake in the preheated oven for 35-40 minutes, or until the filling is set and the top is golden brown.
   2. Let the pie cool slightly before serving.

Quiche Lorraine

Ingredients:

- **For the Pie Crust:**
    - 1 ½ cups all-purpose flour
    - ½ tsp salt
    - 2 tbsp granulated sugar
    - ½ cup (1 stick) unsalted butter, chilled and cut into small cubes
    - 2-4 tbsp ice water
- **For the Filling:**
    - 6 slices bacon, cooked and crumbled
    - 1 cup shredded Gruyère cheese
    - 4 large eggs
    - 1 ¼ cups heavy cream
    - ¼ cup milk
    - ¼ tsp ground nutmeg
    - Salt and pepper to taste

Instructions:

1. **Prepare the Pie Crust:**
    1. In a large bowl, whisk together the flour, salt, and sugar.
    2. Add the chilled butter and use a pastry cutter or your fingers to work it into the flour until the mixture resembles coarse crumbs.
    3. Gradually add the ice water, one tablespoon at a time, mixing until the dough just comes together. Do not overwork.
    4. Flatten the dough into a disk, wrap in plastic wrap, and chill in the refrigerator for at least 30 minutes.
2. **Prepare the Filling:**
    1. Preheat your oven to 375°F (190°C).
    2. Spread the crumbled bacon evenly over the bottom of the pie crust. Sprinkle with shredded Gruyère cheese.
    3. In a large bowl, whisk together the eggs, heavy cream, milk, nutmeg, salt, and pepper.
    4. Pour the egg mixture over the bacon and cheese in the crust.
3. **Bake the Quiche:**

1. Bake in the preheated oven for 35-40 minutes, or until the filling is set and the top is golden brown.
2. Allow to cool slightly before slicing and serving.

Broccoli Cheddar Pie

Ingredients:

- **For the Pie Crust:**
    - 1 ½ cups all-purpose flour
    - ½ tsp salt
    - 2 tbsp granulated sugar
    - ½ cup (1 stick) unsalted butter, chilled and cut into small cubes
    - 2-4 tbsp ice water
- **For the Filling:**
    - 2 cups broccoli florets, steamed and chopped
    - 1 cup shredded cheddar cheese
    - 3 large eggs
    - 1 cup heavy cream
    - ¼ tsp garlic powder
    - Salt and pepper to taste

Instructions:

1. **Prepare the Pie Crust:**
    1. In a large bowl, whisk together the flour, salt, and sugar.
    2. Add the chilled butter and use a pastry cutter or your fingers to work it into the flour until the mixture resembles coarse crumbs.
    3. Gradually add the ice water, one tablespoon at a time, mixing until the dough just comes together. Do not overwork.
    4. Flatten the dough into a disk, wrap in plastic wrap, and chill in the refrigerator for at least 30 minutes.
2. **Prepare the Filling:**
    1. Preheat your oven to 375°F (190°C).
    2. In a large bowl, combine the chopped broccoli and shredded cheddar cheese.
    3. In another bowl, whisk together the eggs, heavy cream, garlic powder, salt, and pepper.
    4. Mix the egg mixture with the broccoli and cheese until well combined.
3. **Assemble the Pie:**
    1. Roll out the chilled dough to fit a 9-inch pie dish. Carefully transfer it to the dish, pressing it into the bottom and up the sides.

    2. Pour the filling into the crust.
4. **Bake the Pie:**
    1. Bake in the preheated oven for 35-40 minutes, or until the filling is set and the top is golden brown.
    2. Let the pie cool slightly before serving.

Tomato Pie

Ingredients:

- **For the Pie Crust:**
    - 1 ½ cups all-purpose flour
    - ½ tsp salt
    - 2 tbsp granulated sugar
    - ½ cup (1 stick) unsalted butter, chilled and cut into small cubes
    - 2-4 tbsp ice water
- **For the Filling:**
    - 4 large ripe tomatoes, sliced
    - 1 cup shredded mozzarella cheese
    - ½ cup mayonnaise
    - ¼ cup grated Parmesan cheese
    - 2 tbsp chopped fresh basil
    - 1 tsp dried oregano
    - Salt and pepper to taste
    - 1 egg, beaten (for egg wash)

Instructions:

1. **Prepare the Pie Crust:**
    1. In a large bowl, whisk together the flour, salt, and sugar.
    2. Add the chilled butter and use a pastry cutter or your fingers to work it into the flour until the mixture resembles coarse crumbs.
    3. Gradually add the ice water, one tablespoon at a time, mixing until the dough just comes together. Do not overwork.
    4. Flatten the dough into a disk, wrap in plastic wrap, and chill in the refrigerator for at least 30 minutes.
2. **Prepare the Filling:**
    1. Preheat your oven to 375°F (190°C).
    2. In a medium bowl, combine the mozzarella cheese, mayonnaise, Parmesan cheese, chopped basil, oregano, salt, and pepper.
    3. Arrange the tomato slices in a single layer on paper towels and sprinkle with a little salt to draw out excess moisture. Pat dry.
3. **Assemble the Pie:**

1. Roll out the chilled dough to fit a 9-inch pie dish. Carefully transfer it to the dish, pressing it into the bottom and up the sides.
2. Spread the cheese mixture evenly over the crust.
3. Arrange the tomato slices on top of the cheese mixture.
4. Brush the edges of the crust with the beaten egg.

4. **Bake the Pie:**
    1. Bake in the preheated oven for 30-35 minutes, or until the crust is golden and the tomatoes are tender.
    2. Allow to cool slightly before serving.

Tofu Pot Pie

Ingredients:

- **For the Pie Crust:**
    - 2 ½ cups all-purpose flour
    - 1 tsp salt
    - 1 tsp sugar
    - 1 cup (2 sticks) unsalted butter, chilled and cut into small cubes
    - 6-8 tbsp ice water
- **For the Filling:**
    - 1 tbsp olive oil
    - 1 small onion, finely chopped
    - 2 cloves garlic, minced
    - 1 cup carrots, diced
    - 1 cup peas
    - 1 cup potatoes, diced
    - 14 oz firm tofu, drained and cubed
    - ¼ cup soy sauce
    - ¼ cup all-purpose flour
    - 1 cup vegetable broth
    - 1 cup almond milk or other non-dairy milk
    - 1 tsp dried thyme
    - 1 tsp dried rosemary
    - Salt and pepper to taste
    - 1 egg, beaten (for egg wash, optional)

Instructions:

1. **Prepare the Pie Crust:**
    1. In a large bowl, whisk together the flour, salt, and sugar.
    2. Add the chilled butter and use a pastry cutter or your fingers to work it into the flour until the mixture resembles coarse crumbs.
    3. Gradually add the ice water, one tablespoon at a time, mixing until the dough just comes together. Do not overwork.
    4. Flatten the dough into two disks, wrap in plastic wrap, and chill in the refrigerator for at least 1 hour.
2. **Prepare the Filling:**

1. Preheat your oven to 425°F (220°C).
2. Heat the olive oil in a large skillet over medium heat. Add the onion and garlic, and cook until softened.
3. Add the carrots and potatoes, and cook until slightly tender.
4. Stir in the tofu and soy sauce, and cook for another 2 minutes.
5. Sprinkle the flour over the mixture and stir to combine.
6. Gradually whisk in the vegetable broth and almond milk. Cook until the mixture thickens.
7. Add the peas, thyme, rosemary, salt, and pepper. Stir to combine.

3. **Assemble the Pie:**
    1. Roll out one disk of dough to fit a 9-inch pie dish. Carefully transfer it to the dish, pressing it into the bottom and up the sides.
    2. Pour the filling into the crust.
    3. Roll out the second disk of dough and place it over the filling. Trim any excess dough and crimp the edges to seal. Cut slits in the top crust for steam to escape.
    4. Brush the top crust with the beaten egg if using.
4. **Bake the Pie:**
    1. Bake in the preheated oven for 45-50 minutes, or until the crust is golden brown and the filling is bubbling.
    2. Let the pie cool for a few minutes before serving.

Pear Pie

Ingredients:

- **For the Pie Crust:**
    - 2 ½ cups all-purpose flour
    - 1 tsp salt
    - 1 tsp sugar
    - 1 cup (2 sticks) unsalted butter, chilled and cut into small cubes
    - 6-8 tbsp ice water
- **For the Filling:**
    - 6-7 ripe pears, peeled, cored, and sliced
    - ¾ cup granulated sugar
    - ¼ cup light brown sugar
    - ¼ cup all-purpose flour
    - 1 tsp ground cinnamon
    - ¼ tsp ground nutmeg
    - 1 tbsp lemon juice
    - 1 egg, beaten (for egg wash)
    - 1 tbsp granulated sugar (for topping)

Instructions:

1. **Prepare the Pie Crust:**
    1. In a large bowl, whisk together the flour, salt, and sugar.
    2. Add the chilled butter and use a pastry cutter or your fingers to work it into the flour until the mixture resembles coarse crumbs.
    3. Gradually add the ice water, one tablespoon at a time, mixing until the dough just comes together. Do not overwork.
    4. Divide the dough into two equal portions, flatten each into a disk, and wrap in plastic wrap. Chill in the refrigerator for at least 1 hour.
2. **Prepare the Filling:**
    1. Preheat your oven to 375°F (190°C).
    2. In a large bowl, toss the sliced pears with granulated sugar, brown sugar, flour, cinnamon, nutmeg, and lemon juice.
3. **Assemble the Pie:**
    1. Roll out one disk of dough to fit a 9-inch pie dish. Carefully transfer it to the dish, pressing it into the bottom and up the sides.

2. Pour the pear mixture into the crust.
3. Roll out the second disk of dough and place it over the filling. Trim any excess dough and crimp the edges to seal. Cut slits in the top crust for steam to escape.
4. Brush the top crust with the beaten egg and sprinkle with granulated sugar.

4. **Bake the Pie:**
    1. Bake in the preheated oven for 45-50 minutes, or until the crust is golden brown and the filling is bubbly.
    2. Allow to cool before serving.

Mixed Berry Pie

Ingredients:

- **For the Pie Crust:**
    - 2 ½ cups all-purpose flour
    - 1 tsp salt
    - 1 tsp sugar
    - 1 cup (2 sticks) unsalted butter, chilled and cut into small cubes
    - 6-8 tbsp ice water
- **For the Filling:**
    - 1 cup strawberries, hulled and sliced
    - 1 cup blueberries
    - 1 cup raspberries
    - ¾ cup granulated sugar
    - ¼ cup cornstarch
    - 1 tsp lemon zest
    - 1 tbsp lemon juice
    - 1 egg, beaten (for egg wash)
    - 1 tbsp granulated sugar (for topping)

Instructions:

1. **Prepare the Pie Crust:**
    1. In a large bowl, whisk together the flour, salt, and sugar.
    2. Add the chilled butter and use a pastry cutter or your fingers to work it into the flour until the mixture resembles coarse crumbs.
    3. Gradually add the ice water, one tablespoon at a time, mixing until the dough just comes together. Do not overwork.
    4. Divide the dough into two equal portions, flatten each into a disk, and wrap in plastic wrap. Chill in the refrigerator for at least 1 hour.
2. **Prepare the Filling:**
    1. Preheat your oven to 375°F (190°C).
    2. In a large bowl, gently toss together the strawberries, blueberries, raspberries, granulated sugar, cornstarch, lemon zest, and lemon juice.
3. **Assemble the Pie:**
    1. Roll out one disk of dough to fit a 9-inch pie dish. Carefully transfer it to the dish, pressing it into the bottom and up the sides.

2. Pour the berry mixture into the crust.
3. Roll out the second disk of dough and place it over the filling. Trim any excess dough and crimp the edges to seal. Cut slits in the top crust for steam to escape.
4. Brush the top crust with the beaten egg and sprinkle with granulated sugar.

4. **Bake the Pie:**
    1. Bake in the preheated oven for 45-50 minutes, or until the crust is golden brown and the filling is bubbly.
    2. Allow to cool before serving.

Custard Pie

Ingredients:

- **For the Pie Crust:**
    - 1 ½ cups all-purpose flour
    - ½ tsp salt
    - 2 tbsp granulated sugar
    - ½ cup (1 stick) unsalted butter, chilled and cut into small cubes
    - 2-4 tbsp ice water
- **For the Custard Filling:**
    - 4 large eggs
    - 1 ¼ cups granulated sugar
    - 1 tsp vanilla extract
    - 1 ¼ cups whole milk
    - 1 ¼ cups heavy cream
    - ¼ tsp ground nutmeg
    - ¼ tsp ground cinnamon

Instructions:

1. **Prepare the Pie Crust:**
    1. In a large bowl, whisk together the flour, salt, and sugar.
    2. Add the chilled butter and use a pastry cutter or your fingers to work it into the flour until the mixture resembles coarse crumbs.
    3. Gradually add the ice water, one tablespoon at a time, mixing until the dough just comes together. Do not overwork.
    4. Flatten the dough into a disk, wrap in plastic wrap, and chill in the refrigerator for at least 30 minutes.
2. **Prepare the Custard Filling:**
    1. Preheat your oven to 350°F (175°C).
    2. In a large bowl, whisk together the eggs and granulated sugar until well combined.
    3. Stir in the vanilla extract, milk, and heavy cream until smooth.
    4. Sprinkle the nutmeg and cinnamon over the mixture and gently stir to combine.
3. **Assemble the Pie:**

    1. Roll out the chilled dough to fit a 9-inch pie dish. Carefully transfer it to the dish, pressing it into the bottom and up the sides.
    2. Pour the custard mixture into the prepared crust.
4. **Bake the Pie:**
    1. Bake in the preheated oven for 50-55 minutes, or until the custard is set and the top is lightly golden.
    2. Allow the pie to cool completely before slicing and serving.

Caramel Apple Pie

Ingredients:

- **For the Pie Crust:**
    - 2 ½ cups all-purpose flour
    - 1 tsp salt
    - 1 tsp sugar
    - 1 cup (2 sticks) unsalted butter, chilled and cut into small cubes
    - 6-8 tbsp ice water
- **For the Filling:**
    - 6-7 medium apples (such as Granny Smith), peeled, cored, and sliced
    - ¾ cup granulated sugar
    - ¼ cup packed brown sugar
    - ¼ cup all-purpose flour
    - 1 tsp ground cinnamon
    - ¼ tsp ground nutmeg
    - ¼ tsp salt
    - 1 tbsp lemon juice
    - ½ cup caramel sauce (store-bought or homemade)
    - 1 egg, beaten (for egg wash)
    - 1 tbsp granulated sugar (for topping)

Instructions:

1. **Prepare the Pie Crust:**
    1. In a large bowl, whisk together the flour, salt, and sugar.
    2. Add the chilled butter and use a pastry cutter or your fingers to work it into the flour until the mixture resembles coarse crumbs.
    3. Gradually add the ice water, one tablespoon at a time, mixing until the dough just comes together. Do not overwork.
    4. Divide the dough into two equal portions, flatten each into a disk, and wrap in plastic wrap. Chill in the refrigerator for at least 1 hour.
2. **Prepare the Filling:**
    1. Preheat your oven to 375°F (190°C).
    2. In a large bowl, toss the apple slices with granulated sugar, brown sugar, flour, cinnamon, nutmeg, salt, and lemon juice.
    3. Stir in the caramel sauce until well combined.

3. **Assemble the Pie:**
    1. Roll out one disk of dough to fit a 9-inch pie dish. Carefully transfer it to the dish, pressing it into the bottom and up the sides.
    2. Pour the apple mixture into the crust.
    3. Roll out the second disk of dough and place it over the filling. Trim any excess dough and crimp the edges to seal. Cut slits in the top crust for steam to escape.
    4. Brush the top crust with the beaten egg and sprinkle with granulated sugar.
4. **Bake the Pie:**
    1. Bake in the preheated oven for 50-60 minutes, or until the crust is golden brown and the filling is bubbly.
    2. Allow the pie to cool before serving. Drizzle with additional caramel sauce if desired.

Ginger Peach Pie

Ingredients:

- **For the Pie Crust:**
    - 2 ½ cups all-purpose flour
    - 1 tsp salt
    - 1 tsp sugar
    - 1 cup (2 sticks) unsalted butter, chilled and cut into small cubes
    - 6-8 tbsp ice water
- **For the Filling:**
    - 6-7 ripe peaches, peeled and sliced
    - ¾ cup granulated sugar
    - ¼ cup packed brown sugar
    - ¼ cup all-purpose flour
    - 1 tsp ground ginger
    - ¼ tsp ground cinnamon
    - ¼ tsp ground nutmeg
    - 1 tbsp lemon juice
    - 1 egg, beaten (for egg wash)
    - 1 tbsp granulated sugar (for topping)

Instructions:

1. **Prepare the Pie Crust:**
    1. In a large bowl, whisk together the flour, salt, and sugar.
    2. Add the chilled butter and use a pastry cutter or your fingers to work it into the flour until the mixture resembles coarse crumbs.
    3. Gradually add the ice water, one tablespoon at a time, mixing until the dough just comes together. Do not overwork.
    4. Divide the dough into two equal portions, flatten each into a disk, and wrap in plastic wrap. Chill in the refrigerator for at least 1 hour.
2. **Prepare the Filling:**
    1. Preheat your oven to 375°F (190°C).
    2. In a large bowl, toss the peach slices with granulated sugar, brown sugar, flour, ginger, cinnamon, nutmeg, and lemon juice.
3. **Assemble the Pie:**

1. Roll out one disk of dough to fit a 9-inch pie dish. Carefully transfer it to the dish, pressing it into the bottom and up the sides.
2. Pour the peach mixture into the crust.
3. Roll out the second disk of dough and place it over the filling. Trim any excess dough and crimp the edges to seal. Cut slits in the top crust for steam to escape.
4. Brush the top crust with the beaten egg and sprinkle with granulated sugar.

4. **Bake the Pie:**
   1. Bake in the preheated oven for 45-50 minutes, or until the crust is golden brown and the filling is bubbly.
   2. Allow the pie to cool before serving.

Blackberry Pie

Ingredients:

- **For the Pie Crust:**
    - 2 ½ cups all-purpose flour
    - 1 tsp salt
    - 1 tsp sugar
    - 1 cup (2 sticks) unsalted butter, chilled and cut into small cubes
    - 6-8 tbsp ice water
- **For the Filling:**
    - 4 cups fresh blackberries
    - ¾ cup granulated sugar
    - ¼ cup cornstarch
    - 1 tbsp lemon juice
    - ¼ tsp ground cinnamon
    - ¼ tsp salt
    - 1 egg, beaten (for egg wash)
    - 1 tbsp granulated sugar (for topping)

Instructions:

1. **Prepare the Pie Crust:**
    1. In a large bowl, whisk together the flour, salt, and sugar.
    2. Add the chilled butter and use a pastry cutter or your fingers to work it into the flour until the mixture resembles coarse crumbs.
    3. Gradually add the ice water, one tablespoon at a time, mixing until the dough just comes together. Do not overwork.
    4. Divide the dough into two equal portions, flatten each into a disk, and wrap in plastic wrap. Chill in the refrigerator for at least 1 hour.
2. **Prepare the Filling:**
    1. Preheat your oven to 375°F (190°C).
    2. In a large bowl, toss the blackberries with granulated sugar, cornstarch, lemon juice, cinnamon, and salt.
3. **Assemble the Pie:**
    1. Roll out one disk of dough to fit a 9-inch pie dish. Carefully transfer it to the dish, pressing it into the bottom and up the sides.
    2. Pour the blackberry mixture into the crust.

3. Roll out the second disk of dough and place it over the filling. Trim any excess dough and crimp the edges to seal. Cut slits in the top crust for steam to escape.
4. Brush the top crust with the beaten egg and sprinkle with granulated sugar.

4. **Bake the Pie:**
    1. Bake in the preheated oven for 45-50 minutes, or until the crust is golden brown and the filling is bubbly.
    2. Allow to cool before serving.

Fig Pie

Ingredients:

- **For the Pie Crust:**
    - 2 ½ cups all-purpose flour
    - 1 tsp salt
    - 1 tsp sugar
    - 1 cup (2 sticks) unsalted butter, chilled and cut into small cubes
    - 6-8 tbsp ice water
- **For the Filling:**
    - 2 cups fresh figs, stemmed and quartered
    - ¾ cup granulated sugar
    - ¼ cup light brown sugar
    - ¼ cup all-purpose flour
    - 1 tsp vanilla extract
    - ¼ tsp ground cinnamon
    - ¼ tsp salt
    - 1 egg, beaten (for egg wash)
    - 1 tbsp granulated sugar (for topping)

Instructions:

1. **Prepare the Pie Crust:**
    1. In a large bowl, whisk together the flour, salt, and sugar.
    2. Add the chilled butter and use a pastry cutter or your fingers to work it into the flour until the mixture resembles coarse crumbs.
    3. Gradually add the ice water, one tablespoon at a time, mixing until the dough just comes together. Do not overwork.
    4. Divide the dough into two equal portions, flatten each into a disk, and wrap in plastic wrap. Chill in the refrigerator for at least 1 hour.
2. **Prepare the Filling:**
    1. Preheat your oven to 375°F (190°C).
    2. In a large bowl, combine the figs with granulated sugar, brown sugar, flour, vanilla extract, cinnamon, and salt.
3. **Assemble the Pie:**
    1. Roll out one disk of dough to fit a 9-inch pie dish. Carefully transfer it to the dish, pressing it into the bottom and up the sides.

2. Pour the fig mixture into the crust.
3. Roll out the second disk of dough and place it over the filling. Trim any excess dough and crimp the edges to seal. Cut slits in the top crust for steam to escape.
4. Brush the top crust with the beaten egg and sprinkle with granulated sugar.

4. **Bake the Pie:**
    1. Bake in the preheated oven for 45-50 minutes, or until the crust is golden brown and the filling is bubbly.
    2. Allow to cool before serving.

Sweet Corn Pie

Ingredients:

- **For the Pie Crust:**
    - 2 ½ cups all-purpose flour
    - 1 tsp salt
    - 1 tsp sugar
    - 1 cup (2 sticks) unsalted butter, chilled and cut into small cubes
    - 6-8 tbsp ice water
- **For the Filling:**
    - 2 cups fresh corn kernels (about 4 ears) or frozen corn, thawed
    - ¾ cup granulated sugar
    - ¼ cup all-purpose flour
    - ¼ tsp salt
    - 3 large eggs
    - 1 cup heavy cream
    - ½ cup milk
    - 1 tsp vanilla extract

Instructions:

1. **Prepare the Pie Crust:**
    1. In a large bowl, whisk together the flour, salt, and sugar.
    2. Add the chilled butter and use a pastry cutter or your fingers to work it into the flour until the mixture resembles coarse crumbs.
    3. Gradually add the ice water, one tablespoon at a time, mixing until the dough just comes together. Do not overwork.
    4. Divide the dough into two equal portions, flatten each into a disk, and wrap in plastic wrap. Chill in the refrigerator for at least 1 hour.
2. **Prepare the Filling:**
    1. Preheat your oven to 350°F (175°C).
    2. In a blender or food processor, pulse the corn kernels until they are slightly pureed but still have some texture.
    3. In a large bowl, combine the pureed corn with granulated sugar, flour, and salt.
    4. Beat in the eggs one at a time, then mix in the heavy cream, milk, and vanilla extract.

3. **Assemble the Pie:**
    1. Roll out one disk of dough to fit a 9-inch pie dish. Carefully transfer it to the dish, pressing it into the bottom and up the sides.
    2. Pour the corn filling into the crust.
4. **Bake the Pie:**
    1. Bake in the preheated oven for 45-50 minutes, or until the filling is set and the top is lightly golden.
    2. Allow the pie to cool before serving.

Egg Custard Pie

Ingredients:

- **For the Pie Crust:**
    - 1 ½ cups all-purpose flour
    - ½ tsp salt
    - 2 tbsp granulated sugar
    - ½ cup (1 stick) unsalted butter, chilled and cut into small cubes
    - 2-4 tbsp ice water
- **For the Custard Filling:**
    - 4 large eggs
    - 1 ¼ cups granulated sugar
    - 1 tsp vanilla extract
    - 1 ¼ cups whole milk
    - 1 ¼ cups heavy cream
    - ¼ tsp ground nutmeg

Instructions:

1. **Prepare the Pie Crust:**
    1. In a large bowl, whisk together the flour, salt, and sugar.
    2. Add the chilled butter and use a pastry cutter or your fingers to work it into the flour until the mixture resembles coarse crumbs.
    3. Gradually add the ice water, one tablespoon at a time, mixing until the dough just comes together. Do not overwork.
    4. Flatten the dough into a disk, wrap in plastic wrap, and chill in the refrigerator for at least 30 minutes.
2. **Prepare the Custard Filling:**
    1. Preheat your oven to 350°F (175°C).
    2. In a large bowl, whisk together the eggs and granulated sugar until well combined.
    3. Stir in the vanilla extract, milk, and heavy cream until smooth.
    4. Sprinkle the nutmeg over the top of the mixture.
3. **Assemble the Pie:**
    1. Roll out the chilled dough to fit a 9-inch pie dish. Carefully transfer it to the dish, pressing it into the bottom and up the sides.
    2. Pour the custard mixture into the prepared crust.

4. **Bake the Pie:**
    1. Bake in the preheated oven for 50-55 minutes, or until the custard is set and the top is lightly golden.
    2. Allow the pie to cool completely before slicing and serving.

Almond Cream Pie

Ingredients:

- **For the Pie Crust:**
    - 1 ½ cups all-purpose flour
    - ½ tsp salt
    - 2 tbsp granulated sugar
    - ½ cup (1 stick) unsalted butter, chilled and cut into small cubes
    - 2-4 tbsp ice water
- **For the Filling:**
    - 1 cup heavy cream
    - ½ cup almond milk
    - ⅓ cup granulated sugar
    - 3 large egg yolks
    - 2 tbsp cornstarch
    - ½ cup almond paste, crumbled
    - 1 tsp almond extract
    - Sliced almonds, for garnish

Instructions:

1. **Prepare the Pie Crust:**
    1. In a large bowl, whisk together the flour, salt, and sugar.
    2. Add the chilled butter and use a pastry cutter or your fingers to work it into the flour until the mixture resembles coarse crumbs.
    3. Gradually add the ice water, one tablespoon at a time, mixing until the dough just comes together. Do not overwork.
    4. Flatten the dough into a disk, wrap in plastic wrap, and chill in the refrigerator for at least 30 minutes.
2. **Prepare the Filling:**
    1. Preheat your oven to 350°F (175°C).
    2. In a medium saucepan, combine the heavy cream, almond milk, and granulated sugar. Heat over medium heat until just about to simmer.
    3. In a separate bowl, whisk the egg yolks and cornstarch until smooth. Gradually add some of the hot cream mixture to the egg yolks, whisking constantly.

4. Return the egg mixture to the saucepan and cook, whisking constantly, until the mixture thickens.
5. Remove from heat and stir in the crumbled almond paste and almond extract until smooth.

3. **Assemble the Pie:**
    1. Roll out the chilled dough to fit a 9-inch pie dish. Carefully transfer it to the dish, pressing it into the bottom and up the sides.
    2. Bake the crust in the preheated oven for 15-20 minutes, or until lightly golden. Allow to cool completely.
    3. Pour the almond cream filling into the cooled crust and smooth the top.

4. **Garnish and Serve:**
    1. Garnish with sliced almonds.
    2. Chill in the refrigerator for at least 2 hours before serving.

Lemon Chess Pie

Ingredients:

- **For the Pie Crust:**
    - 1 ½ cups all-purpose flour
    - ½ tsp salt
    - 2 tbsp granulated sugar
    - ½ cup (1 stick) unsalted butter, chilled and cut into small cubes
    - 2-4 tbsp ice water
- **For the Filling:**
    - 1 ¼ cups granulated sugar
    - ¼ cup all-purpose flour
    - ¼ tsp salt
    - 3 large eggs
    - ½ cup melted butter
    - 2 tbsp lemon juice
    - 1 tbsp lemon zest
    - ½ tsp vanilla extract

Instructions:

1. **Prepare the Pie Crust:**
    1. In a large bowl, whisk together the flour, salt, and sugar.
    2. Add the chilled butter and use a pastry cutter or your fingers to work it into the flour until the mixture resembles coarse crumbs.
    3. Gradually add the ice water, one tablespoon at a time, mixing until the dough just comes together. Do not overwork.
    4. Flatten the dough into a disk, wrap in plastic wrap, and chill in the refrigerator for at least 30 minutes.
2. **Prepare the Filling:**
    1. Preheat your oven to 350°F (175°C).
    2. In a large bowl, whisk together the sugar, flour, and salt.
    3. Beat in the eggs one at a time, then stir in the melted butter, lemon juice, lemon zest, and vanilla extract.
3. **Assemble the Pie:**
    1. Roll out the chilled dough to fit a 9-inch pie dish. Carefully transfer it to the dish, pressing it into the bottom and up the sides.

2. Pour the lemon filling into the prepared crust.
4. **Bake the Pie:**
    1. Bake in the preheated oven for 45-50 minutes, or until the filling is set and the top is lightly golden.
    2. Allow the pie to cool before serving.

Poppy Seed Pie

Ingredients:

- **For the Pie Crust:**
    - 2 ½ cups all-purpose flour
    - 1 tsp salt
    - 1 tsp sugar
    - 1 cup (2 sticks) unsalted butter, chilled and cut into small cubes
    - 6-8 tbsp ice water
- **For the Filling:**
    - 1 cup poppy seeds
    - 1 cup milk
    - ¾ cup granulated sugar
    - ½ cup honey
    - 3 large eggs
    - 1 tsp vanilla extract
    - ¼ cup all-purpose flour
    - ¼ tsp salt
    - 1 tbsp lemon juice

Instructions:

1. **Prepare the Pie Crust:**
    1. In a large bowl, whisk together the flour, salt, and sugar.
    2. Add the chilled butter and use a pastry cutter or your fingers to work it into the flour until the mixture resembles coarse crumbs.
    3. Gradually add the ice water, one tablespoon at a time, mixing until the dough just comes together. Do not overwork.
    4. Divide the dough into two equal portions, flatten each into a disk, and wrap in plastic wrap. Chill in the refrigerator for at least 1 hour.
2. **Prepare the Filling:**
    1. Preheat your oven to 350°F (175°C).
    2. In a saucepan, combine the milk, sugar, and honey. Heat until the sugar dissolves and the mixture is hot but not boiling.
    3. In a bowl, whisk together the eggs, vanilla extract, flour, salt, and lemon juice. Gradually add the hot milk mixture, whisking continuously.
    4. Stir in the poppy seeds.

3. **Assemble the Pie:**
    1. Roll out one disk of dough to fit a 9-inch pie dish. Carefully transfer it to the dish, pressing it into the bottom and up the sides.
    2. Pour the poppy seed filling into the crust.
4. **Bake the Pie:**
    1. Bake in the preheated oven for 45-50 minutes, or until the filling is set and the top is golden.
    2. Allow the pie to cool before serving.

Chocolate Peanut Butter Pie

Ingredients:

- **For the Crust:**
    - 1 ½ cups graham cracker crumbs
    - ¼ cup granulated sugar
    - 6 tbsp unsalted butter, melted
- **For the Filling:**
    - 1 cup creamy peanut butter
    - 8 oz cream cheese, softened
    - 1 cup powdered sugar
    - 1 tsp vanilla extract
    - 1 cup heavy cream
    - 6 oz semisweet chocolate, chopped
    - 2 tbsp unsalted butter

Instructions:

1. **Prepare the Crust:**
    1. Preheat your oven to 350°F (175°C).
    2. In a medium bowl, combine the graham cracker crumbs, granulated sugar, and melted butter. Mix until the crumbs are evenly coated.
    3. Press the mixture into the bottom and up the sides of a 9-inch pie dish.
    4. Bake for 8-10 minutes, then let it cool completely.
2. **Prepare the Peanut Butter Filling:**
    1. In a large bowl, beat together the peanut butter, cream cheese, powdered sugar, and vanilla extract until smooth.
    2. In a separate bowl, whip the heavy cream until stiff peaks form. Gently fold the whipped cream into the peanut butter mixture.
    3. Spoon the filling into the cooled crust and smooth the top.
3. **Prepare the Chocolate Ganache:**
    1. In a small saucepan, melt the chocolate and butter over low heat, stirring constantly until smooth.
    2. Let the ganache cool slightly before pouring it over the peanut butter filling.
4. **Chill and Serve:**
    1. Refrigerate the pie for at least 2 hours, or until the ganache is set.

2. Garnish with additional whipped cream or chopped peanuts if desired before serving.

Peanut Butter Pie

Ingredients:

- **For the Crust:**
    - 1 ½ cups crushed graham crackers
    - ¼ cup granulated sugar
    - 6 tbsp unsalted butter, melted
- **For the Filling:**
    - 1 cup creamy peanut butter
    - 8 oz cream cheese, softened
    - 1 cup powdered sugar
    - 1 tsp vanilla extract
    - 1 cup heavy cream

Instructions:

1. **Prepare the Crust:**
    1. Preheat your oven to 350°F (175°C).
    2. In a medium bowl, mix the crushed graham crackers, granulated sugar, and melted butter until the crumbs are evenly coated.
    3. Press the mixture into the bottom and up the sides of a 9-inch pie dish.
    4. Bake for 8-10 minutes, then let it cool completely.
2. **Prepare the Filling:**
    1. In a large bowl, beat together the peanut butter, cream cheese, powdered sugar, and vanilla extract until smooth.
    2. In a separate bowl, whip the heavy cream until stiff peaks form. Gently fold the whipped cream into the peanut butter mixture.
    3. Spoon the filling into the cooled crust and smooth the top.
3. **Chill and Serve:**
    1. Refrigerate the pie for at least 2 hours before serving.
    2. Garnish with additional whipped cream or chopped peanuts if desired.

Apricot Pie

Ingredients:

- **For the Pie Crust:**
    - 2 ½ cups all-purpose flour
    - 1 tsp salt
    - 1 tsp sugar
    - 1 cup (2 sticks) unsalted butter, chilled and cut into small cubes
    - 6-8 tbsp ice water
- **For the Filling:**
    - 4 cups fresh apricots, pitted and sliced
    - ¾ cup granulated sugar
    - ¼ cup light brown sugar
    - ¼ cup all-purpose flour
    - ¼ tsp ground cinnamon
    - ¼ tsp salt
    - 1 tbsp lemon juice
    - 1 egg, beaten (for egg wash)
    - 1 tbsp granulated sugar (for topping)

Instructions:

1. **Prepare the Pie Crust:**
    1. In a large bowl, whisk together the flour, salt, and sugar.
    2. Add the chilled butter and use a pastry cutter or your fingers to work it into the flour until the mixture resembles coarse crumbs.
    3. Gradually add the ice water, one tablespoon at a time, mixing until the dough just comes together. Do not overwork.
    4. Divide the dough into two equal portions, flatten each into a disk, and wrap in plastic wrap. Chill in the refrigerator for at least 1 hour.
2. **Prepare the Filling:**
    1. Preheat your oven to 375°F (190°C).
    2. In a large bowl, combine the apricot slices with granulated sugar, brown sugar, flour, cinnamon, salt, and lemon juice.
3. **Assemble the Pie:**
    1. Roll out one disk of dough to fit a 9-inch pie dish. Carefully transfer it to the dish, pressing it into the bottom and up the sides.

2. Pour the apricot mixture into the crust.
   3. Roll out the second disk of dough and place it over the filling. Trim any excess dough and crimp the edges to seal. Cut slits in the top crust for steam to escape.
   4. Brush the top crust with the beaten egg and sprinkle with granulated sugar.
4. **Bake the Pie:**
   1. Bake in the preheated oven for 45-50 minutes, or until the crust is golden brown and the filling is bubbly.
   2. Allow the pie to cool before serving.

Chocolate Bourbon Pecan Pie

Ingredients:

- **For the Pie Crust:**
    - 1 ½ cups all-purpose flour
    - ½ tsp salt
    - 2 tbsp granulated sugar
    - ½ cup (1 stick) unsalted butter, chilled and cut into small cubes
    - 2-4 tbsp ice water
- **For the Filling:**
    - 1 cup pecan halves
    - ¾ cup granulated sugar
    - ½ cup light corn syrup
    - ¼ cup unsweetened cocoa powder
    - ¼ cup bourbon
    - 4 large eggs
    - 4 tbsp unsalted butter, melted
    - 1 tsp vanilla extract
    - ¼ tsp salt

Instructions:

1. **Prepare the Pie Crust:**
    1. In a large bowl, whisk together the flour, salt, and sugar.
    2. Add the chilled butter and use a pastry cutter or your fingers to work it into the flour until the mixture resembles coarse crumbs.
    3. Gradually add the ice water, one tablespoon at a time, mixing until the dough just comes together. Do not overwork.
    4. Flatten the dough into a disk, wrap in plastic wrap, and chill in the refrigerator for at least 30 minutes.
2. **Prepare the Filling:**
    1. Preheat your oven to 350°F (175°C).
    2. In a medium bowl, whisk together the granulated sugar, corn syrup, cocoa powder, bourbon, eggs, melted butter, vanilla extract, and salt until smooth.
    3. Stir in the pecan halves.
3. **Assemble the Pie:**

1. Roll out the chilled dough to fit a 9-inch pie dish. Carefully transfer it to the dish, pressing it into the bottom and up the sides.
   2. Pour the pecan filling into the crust.
4. **Bake the Pie:**
   1. Bake in the preheated oven for 50-55 minutes, or until the filling is set and the top is glossy.
   2. Allow the pie to cool before serving.

Maple Cream Pie

Ingredients:

- **For the Pie Crust:**
    - 1 ½ cups graham cracker crumbs
    - ¼ cup granulated sugar
    - 6 tbsp unsalted butter, melted
- **For the Filling:**
    - 1 cup pure maple syrup
    - ¼ cup all-purpose flour
    - 1 cup heavy cream
    - 3 large egg yolks
    - ¼ tsp salt
    - 1 tsp vanilla extract

Instructions:

1. **Prepare the Crust:**
    1. Preheat your oven to 350°F (175°C).
    2. In a medium bowl, combine the graham cracker crumbs, granulated sugar, and melted butter. Mix until the crumbs are evenly coated.
    3. Press the mixture into the bottom and up the sides of a 9-inch pie dish.
    4. Bake for 8-10 minutes, then let it cool completely.
2. **Prepare the Filling:**
    1. In a medium saucepan, heat the maple syrup over medium heat until it begins to simmer.
    2. In a bowl, whisk together the flour and egg yolks until smooth.
    3. Gradually add some of the hot syrup to the egg yolks, whisking constantly to temper.
    4. Return the mixture to the saucepan and cook, whisking constantly, until thickened.
    5. Remove from heat and stir in the heavy cream, salt, and vanilla extract.
3. **Assemble the Pie:**
    1. Pour the maple cream filling into the cooled crust.
4. **Chill and Serve:**
    1. Refrigerate the pie for at least 2 hours before serving.
    2. Garnish with whipped cream if desired.

Orange Cream Pie

Ingredients:

- **For the Pie Crust:**
    - 1 ½ cups all-purpose flour
    - ½ tsp salt
    - 2 tbsp granulated sugar
    - ½ cup (1 stick) unsalted butter, chilled and cut into small cubes
    - 2-4 tbsp ice water
- **For the Filling:**
    - 1 cup orange juice
    - 2 tbsp cornstarch
    - ½ cup granulated sugar
    - 3 large egg yolks
    - 1 cup heavy cream
    - 1 tsp orange zest
    - 1 tsp vanilla extract

Instructions:

1. **Prepare the Pie Crust:**
    1. In a large bowl, whisk together the flour, salt, and sugar.
    2. Add the chilled butter and use a pastry cutter or your

fingers to work it into the flour until the mixture resembles coarse crumbs. 3. Gradually add the ice water, one tablespoon at a time, mixing until the dough just comes together. Do not overwork. 4. Flatten the dough into a disk, wrap in plastic wrap, and chill in the refrigerator for at least 30 minutes. 2. **Prepare the Filling:**

1. Preheat your oven to 350°F (175°C).
2. In a medium saucepan, combine the orange juice and cornstarch. Heat over medium heat, whisking constantly until the mixture begins to thicken.
3. In a separate bowl, whisk together the granulated sugar and egg yolks.
4. Gradually whisk the hot orange mixture into the egg yolks, then return the mixture to the saucepan.
5. Cook, whisking constantly, until the filling is thick and bubbly. Remove from heat and stir in the heavy cream, orange zest, and vanilla extract.

6. **Assemble the Pie:**
    1. Roll out the chilled dough to fit a 9-inch pie dish. Carefully transfer it to the dish, pressing it into the bottom and up the sides.
    2. Bake the crust in the preheated oven for 15-20 minutes, or until lightly golden. Allow to cool completely.
    3. Pour the orange cream filling into the cooled crust.
7. **Chill and Serve:**
    1. Refrigerate the pie for at least 2 hours before serving.
    2. Garnish with whipped cream and additional orange zest if desired.

Almond Raspberry Pie

Ingredients:

- **For the Pie Crust:**
    - 2 ½ cups all-purpose flour
    - 1 tsp salt
    - 1 tsp sugar
    - 1 cup (2 sticks) unsalted butter, chilled and cut into small cubes
    - 6-8 tbsp ice water
- **For the Filling:**
    - 1 cup raspberry preserves
    - 1 cup fresh raspberries
    - ½ cup almond paste, crumbled
    - ½ cup granulated sugar
    - ¼ cup all-purpose flour
    - 1 tsp almond extract
    - 1 egg, beaten (for egg wash)
    - Sliced almonds, for topping

Instructions:

1. **Prepare the Pie Crust:**
    1. In a large bowl, whisk together the flour, salt, and sugar.
    2. Add the chilled butter and use a pastry cutter or your fingers to work it into the flour until the mixture resembles coarse crumbs.
    3. Gradually add the ice water, one tablespoon at a time, mixing until the dough just comes together. Do not overwork.
    4. Divide the dough into two equal portions, flatten each into a disk, and wrap in plastic wrap. Chill in the refrigerator for at least 1 hour.
2. **Prepare the Filling:**
    1. Preheat your oven to 375°F (190°C).
    2. In a large bowl, combine the raspberry preserves, fresh raspberries, almond paste, granulated sugar, flour, and almond extract. Mix until well combined.
3. **Assemble the Pie:**
    1. Roll out one disk of dough to fit a 9-inch pie dish. Carefully transfer it to the dish, pressing it into the bottom and up the sides.

2. Pour the raspberry mixture into the crust.
   3. Roll out the second disk of dough and place it over the filling. Trim any excess dough and crimp the edges to seal. Cut slits in the top crust for steam to escape.
   4. Brush the top crust with the beaten egg and sprinkle with sliced almonds.
4. **Bake the Pie:**
   1. Bake in the preheated oven for 45-50 minutes, or until the crust is golden brown and the filling is bubbly.
   2. Allow the pie to cool before serving.

Zucchini Pie

Ingredients:

- **For the Pie Crust:**
    - 1 ½ cups all-purpose flour
    - ½ tsp salt
    - 2 tbsp granulated sugar
    - ½ cup (1 stick) unsalted butter, chilled and cut into small cubes
    - 2-4 tbsp ice water
- **For the Filling:**
    - 2 cups grated zucchini, drained
    - 1 cup shredded cheddar cheese
    - ½ cup finely chopped onion
    - ½ cup sour cream
    - 3 large eggs
    - 1/3 cup mayonnaise
    - 1 tsp dried thyme
    - ¼ tsp garlic powder
    - Salt and pepper to taste

Instructions:

1. **Prepare the Pie Crust:**
    1. In a large bowl, whisk together the flour, salt, and sugar.
    2. Add the chilled butter and use a pastry cutter or your fingers to work it into the flour until the mixture resembles coarse crumbs.
    3. Gradually add the ice water, one tablespoon at a time, mixing until the dough just comes together. Do not overwork.
    4. Flatten the dough into a disk, wrap in plastic wrap, and chill in the refrigerator for at least 30 minutes.
2. **Prepare the Filling:**
    1. Preheat your oven to 375°F (190°C).
    2. In a large bowl, combine the grated zucchini, cheddar cheese, chopped onion, sour cream, eggs, mayonnaise, thyme, garlic powder, salt, and pepper. Mix well.
3. **Assemble the Pie:**

    1. Roll out the chilled dough to fit a 9-inch pie dish. Carefully transfer it to the dish, pressing it into the bottom and up the sides.
    2. Pour the zucchini mixture into the crust and spread evenly.
4. **Bake the Pie:**
    1. Bake in the preheated oven for 35-40 minutes, or until the filling is set and the top is golden brown.
    2. Allow the pie to cool slightly before serving.

Tomato Basil Pie

Ingredients:

- **For the Pie Crust:**
    - 1 ½ cups all-purpose flour
    - ½ tsp salt
    - 2 tbsp granulated sugar
    - ½ cup (1 stick) unsalted butter, chilled and cut into small cubes
    - 2-4 tbsp ice water
- **For the Filling:**
    - 2 cups sliced tomatoes (about 4 medium tomatoes)
    - 1 cup shredded mozzarella cheese
    - ½ cup mayonnaise
    - ½ cup grated Parmesan cheese
    - ¼ cup chopped fresh basil (or 1 tbsp dried basil)
    - 1 tbsp olive oil
    - 1 tsp dried oregano
    - Salt and pepper to taste

Instructions:

1. **Prepare the Pie Crust:**
    1. In a large bowl, whisk together the flour, salt, and sugar.
    2. Add the chilled butter and use a pastry cutter or your fingers to work it into the flour until the mixture resembles coarse crumbs.
    3. Gradually add the ice water, one tablespoon at a time, mixing until the dough just comes together. Do not overwork.
    4. Flatten the dough into a disk, wrap in plastic wrap, and chill in the refrigerator for at least 30 minutes.
2. **Prepare the Filling:**
    1. Preheat your oven to 375°F (190°C).
    2. In a medium bowl, mix together the mozzarella cheese, mayonnaise, Parmesan cheese, basil, olive oil, oregano, salt, and pepper.
    3. Slice the tomatoes and arrange them on a paper towel to drain excess moisture.
3. **Assemble the Pie:**

1. Roll out the chilled dough to fit a 9-inch pie dish. Carefully transfer it to the dish, pressing it into the bottom and up the sides.
2. Spread the cheese mixture evenly over the crust.
3. Arrange the tomato slices on top of the cheese mixture, slightly overlapping them.

4. **Bake the Pie:**
    1. Bake in the preheated oven for 40-45 minutes, or until the crust is golden and the filling is bubbly.
    2. Allow the pie to cool slightly before serving.

Honey Pie

Ingredients:

- **For the Pie Crust:**
    - 1 ½ cups all-purpose flour
    - ½ tsp salt
    - 2 tbsp granulated sugar
    - ½ cup (1 stick) unsalted butter, chilled and cut into small cubes
    - 2-4 tbsp ice water
- **For the Filling:**
    - 1 cup pure honey
    - 3 large eggs
    - ½ cup heavy cream
    - ¼ cup whole milk
    - 1 tsp vanilla extract
    - ¼ tsp salt
    - 1 tbsp all-purpose flour

Instructions:

1. **Prepare the Pie Crust:**
    1. In a large bowl, whisk together the flour, salt, and sugar.
    2. Add the chilled butter and use a pastry cutter or your fingers to work it into the flour until the mixture resembles coarse crumbs.
    3. Gradually add the ice water, one tablespoon at a time, mixing until the dough just comes together. Do not overwork.
    4. Flatten the dough into a disk, wrap in plastic wrap, and chill in the refrigerator for at least 30 minutes.
2. **Prepare the Filling:**
    1. Preheat your oven to 350°F (175°C).
    2. In a medium bowl, whisk together the honey, eggs, heavy cream, milk, vanilla extract, salt, and flour until smooth.
3. **Assemble the Pie:**
    1. Roll out the chilled dough to fit a 9-inch pie dish. Carefully transfer it to the dish, pressing it into the bottom and up the sides.
    2. Pour the honey mixture into the crust.
4. **Bake the Pie:**

1. Bake in the preheated oven for 45-50 minutes, or until the filling is set and slightly golden around the edges.
2. Allow the pie to cool before serving.

Butterscotch Pie

Ingredients:

- **For the Pie Crust:**
    - 1 ½ cups graham cracker crumbs
    - ¼ cup granulated sugar
    - 6 tbsp unsalted butter, melted
- **For the Filling:**
    - 1 cup packed brown sugar
    - ¼ cup unsalted butter
    - ¼ cup all-purpose flour
    - 2 cups whole milk
    - 4 large egg yolks
    - 1 tsp vanilla extract
    - Pinch of salt
- **For the Topping:**
    - Whipped cream
    - Optional: extra butterscotch sauce for drizzling

Instructions:

1. **Prepare the Crust:**
    1. Preheat your oven to 350°F (175°C).
    2. In a medium bowl, combine the graham cracker crumbs, granulated sugar, and melted butter. Mix until the crumbs are evenly coated.
    3. Press the mixture into the bottom and up the sides of a 9-inch pie dish.
    4. Bake for 8-10 minutes, then let it cool completely.
2. **Prepare the Filling:**
    1. In a medium saucepan, melt the butter over medium heat. Add the brown sugar and cook, stirring frequently, until the sugar is fully dissolved and the mixture is bubbly.
    2. Stir in the flour and cook for 1 minute, continuing to stir.
    3. Gradually whisk in the milk and cook until the mixture thickens and begins to bubble.
    4. In a separate bowl, lightly beat the egg yolks. Slowly add a small amount of the hot mixture to the egg yolks to temper them, then return the egg mixture to the saucepan.

5. Cook for an additional 2 minutes, stirring constantly.
   6. Remove from heat and stir in the vanilla extract and a pinch of salt.
   7. Pour the butterscotch filling into the cooled pie crust.
3. **Chill and Serve:**
   1. Refrigerate the pie for at least 2 hours, or until set.
   2. Top with whipped cream before serving. Drizzle with extra butterscotch sauce if desired.

S'mores Pie

Ingredients:

- **For the Crust:**
    - 1 ½ cups graham cracker crumbs
    - ¼ cup granulated sugar
    - 6 tbsp unsalted butter, melted
- **For the Filling:**
    - 1 cup semi-sweet chocolate chips
    - ½ cup heavy cream
    - ½ cup marshmallow fluff
    - ¼ cup mini marshmallows
    - Optional: crushed graham crackers for garnish

Instructions:

1. **Prepare the Crust:**
    1. Preheat your oven to 350°F (175°C).
    2. In a medium bowl, mix together the graham cracker crumbs, granulated sugar, and melted butter until evenly coated.
    3. Press the mixture into the bottom and up the sides of a 9-inch pie dish.
    4. Bake for 8-10 minutes, then let it cool completely.
2. **Prepare the Filling:**
    1. In a small saucepan, heat the heavy cream over medium heat until it begins to simmer.
    2. Remove from heat and stir in the chocolate chips until fully melted and smooth.
    3. Pour the chocolate mixture into the cooled crust and spread evenly.
    4. Refrigerate until set, about 1 hour.
3. **Add the Marshmallow Layer:**
    1. Once the chocolate layer is set, spread the marshmallow fluff over the top.
    2. Preheat your oven's broiler. Place the pie under the broiler for about 1-2 minutes, or until the marshmallows are lightly toasted. Watch closely to prevent burning.
4. **Garnish and Serve:**
    1. Sprinkle with crushed graham crackers if desired.
    2. Allow the pie to cool slightly before serving.

Key Lime Cheesecake Pie

Ingredients:

- **For the Crust:**
    - 1 ½ cups graham cracker crumbs
    - ¼ cup granulated sugar
    - 6 tbsp unsalted butter, melted
- **For the Filling:**
    - 1 cup key lime juice (fresh or bottled)
    - 1 cup granulated sugar
    - 16 oz cream cheese, softened
    - 1 cup sour cream
    - 3 large eggs
    - 1 tsp vanilla extract
- **For the Topping:**
    - Whipped cream
    - Lime zest for garnish

Instructions:

1. **Prepare the Crust:**
    1. Preheat your oven to 350°F (175°C).
    2. In a medium bowl, combine the graham cracker crumbs, granulated sugar, and melted butter. Mix until the crumbs are evenly coated.
    3. Press the mixture into the bottom and up the sides of a 9-inch pie dish.
    4. Bake for 8-10 minutes, then let it cool completely.
2. **Prepare the Filling:**
    1. In a large bowl, beat the cream cheese until smooth.
    2. Gradually add the sugar and continue to beat until fully combined.
    3. Add the sour cream, key lime juice, eggs, and vanilla extract. Beat until smooth and well combined.
    4. Pour the filling into the cooled crust.
3. **Bake the Pie:**
    1. Bake in the preheated oven for 45-50 minutes, or until the center is set and the edges are lightly browned.
    2. Turn off the oven and let the pie cool inside with the door slightly ajar for 1 hour.

    3. Refrigerate for at least 4 hours, or overnight, to chill and set.
4. **Serve:**
    1. Top with whipped cream and garnish with lime zest before serving.

www.ingramcontent.com/pod-product-compliance
Lightning Source LLC
LaVergne TN
LVHW081604060526
838201LV00054B/2072